SAVE THE PANDA

Sarah Eason

PowerKiDS press.

New York

Published in 2009 by The Rosen Publishing Group, Inc.
29 East 21st Street, New York, NY 10010

Copyright © 2009 Bookmart Limited

Illustrators: Andrew Geeson and Marijke Van Veldhoven
Designer: Paul Myerscough
Consultant: Michael Scott
U.S. Editor: Kara Murray

Photo Credits: Ardea/John Cancalosi front cover; Dreamstime/Ge Gao p. 7 /Feng Hui p. 8 /Kim Pin Tan p. 9 /Rudolf Kotulán p. 20 /Natspel p. 27; FLPA/Gerry Ellis/Minden Pictures p. 17 /Katherine Feng/GLOBIO/Minden Pictures p. 22, p. 23, p. 24; Fotolia p. 11 /Clarence Alford p. 19; istockphoto p. 14, p. 15, p. 16, p. 18, p. 25, p. 28; Photolibrary/Oxford Scientific Films /Animals Animals/Ralph Reinhold p. 21 /Oxford Scientific Films/Animals Animals/Lynne Stone p.6 /Oxford Scientific Films/Mike Powles p. 12; Shutterstock p. 13, p. 26 /Olga Bogatyrenko p. 10 /Fenghui p. 4 /Mike Flippo poster /Ravshan Mirzaitov p. 5 /Goydenko Tatiana p. 29.

Library of Congress Cataloging-in-Publication Data

Eason, Sarah.
  Save the panda / Sarah Eason. — 1st ed.
      p. cm. — (Save the)
  Includes index.
  ISBN 978-1-4358-2812-4 (library binding)
  1. Giant panda—Juvenile literature. 2. Pandas—Juvenile literature. I. Title.
  QL737.C214E24 2009
  599.789—dc22

                                        2008025727

Printed in China

Contents

Why Are Pandas So Special?

Pandas are called living fossils because they have lived on Earth for such a long time. They have been here for 3 million years! Yet, although pandas have survived on our planet for so long, they are now one of the most endangered animals on Earth.

SAVE THE PANDA!

There are many things that you can do to help save the panda. Look out for the Save the Panda boxes in this book for ways in which you and your friends can help.

Pandas are very unusual animals. They are called bears but, unlike bears, they do not hibernate. Pandas are also called carnivores, which means meat eaters. However, they eat very little meat and mainly eat **bamboo**.

We are very good at climbing trees. We can also swim.

I live until I am 20 years old.

•• Pandas are very shy animals. They also live in difficult to reach areas, so wild pandas are rarely seen.

Did You Know?

Only 1,600 pandas still live in the wild.

Why Are Pandas in Danger?

We are sometimes killed by traps

Pandas are under threat because people are cutting down the forests in which they live. Bamboo and trees are cut down for wood. The land on which they grew is turned into towns and farmland. **Poachers** also hunt pandas for their fur. The fur is sold and used to make rugs.

SAVE THE PANDA!

You can help save pandas by joining an organization **that protects their** habitat.

Sometimes all the bamboo in one area of a forest dies. Then pandas must travel long distances to find new bamboo. Many forest areas around panda **territory** have now been built on. Pandas cannot travel across these areas. If they cannot travel to find food, they may starve.

This mountain area was once covered in trees and bamboo. The forest has been cut down to make way for roads.

left by hunters to catch musk deer and black bears.

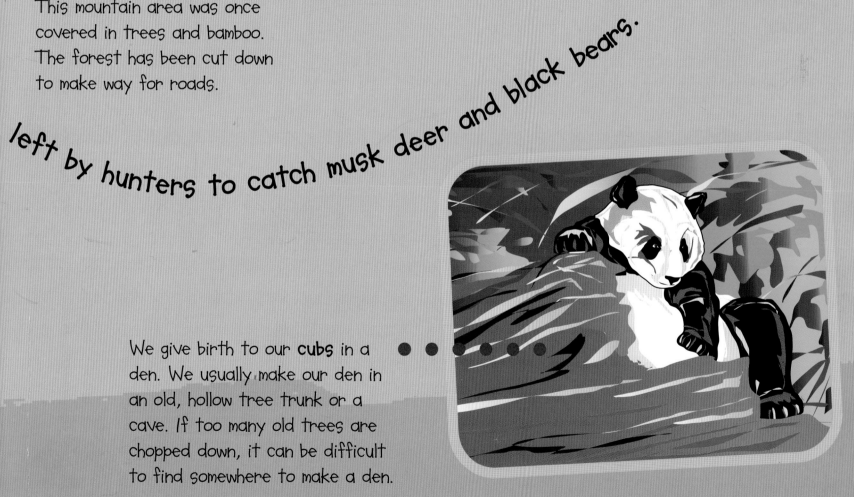

We give birth to our **cubs** in a den. We usually make our den in an old, hollow tree trunk or a cave. If too many old trees are chopped down, it can be difficult to find somewhere to make a den.

Where Do Pandas Live?

Giant pandas live high up in the cold mountain forests of central China. The forests reach high above **sea level**. They touch the clouds and are covered with mist.

It gets very cold in the

Bamboo grows very well in the forests where pandas live. It grows in thick clumps and can reach up to 10 feet (3 m) high.

We are suited to living in cold and damp mountain forests. We feed on bamboo that grows there.

mountain forests. The ground is often covered in deep snow.

China

Mongolia

China

India

South China Sea

We once lived all over Southeast China. Today, we live only in very small mountain areas. The places where pandas once lived are shown in green on this map. The places where they live today are shown in red.

What Do Pandas Look Like?

For many years some **scientists** thought that pandas were bears. Others thought they were more like **raccoons**. Many scientists now think that pandas are neither of these. They believe they are an animal group all their own.

thick hair on feet protects panda when it walks on snow

thick black and white fur

I am the height of a pony when

very good eyesight

short, strong legs carry a heavy body and are used for climbing

powerful jaws for chewing bamboo

long sharp claws

If I sense danger, I can quickly swim across a river or climb a tree to reach safety. I use my strong front legs and long, sharp claws to climb.

Pandas have thick black and white fur. Their fur has an oily, **waterproof** coating, which keeps them dry in their damp, misty home. Pandas are smaller than bears. They also have a rounder face and strong jaws. Their wide, flat teeth are used to chew and grind bamboo.

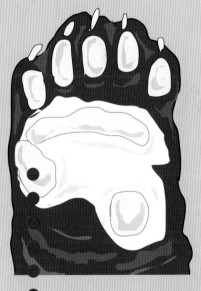

I stand on all fours.

Did You Know?

The Chinese word for panda is xiongmao. It means "giant cat bear."

I have a bone on my wrist that is a little like a thumb. It helps me grip bamboo when I eat.

Where Do Pandas Make Their Home?

The area in which a panda lives is called its habitat. Pandas sleep outside in the open air. When it rains heavily, they take shelter inside a hollow tree trunk or a cave. Pandas live alone – they need a large forest area to themselves in which they can find enough bamboo.

SAVE THE PANDA!

Why not do a walk for charity **to raise money for organizations that protect pandas?**

I make my home

Pandas mark their habitat with **scent**. They spray urine and rub scent on bushes, trees and rocks to tell other pandas to stay away.

Pandas need to find a lot of bamboo to eat every day.

where there is a lot of bamboo and plenty of freshwater.

I spend most of my time in one small area of forest. It is called my core area. I am scratching this tree to show other pandas that this is my home.

Did You Know?

I have a special scent gland under my tail. I rub it on rocks and trees to mark my territory.

What Do Pandas Eat?

Pandas mainly eat bamboo shoots. Their favorite types of bamboo are arrow bamboo, umbrella bamboo and golden bamboo. Pandas sometimes eat herbs, bulbs, tree bark, mice, insects and lizards. They also eat any dead animals they find.

Did You Know?

I eat a quarter of my body weight in bamboo every day!

My stomach has

14

I use my teeth and rough tongue to strip the leaves and tough outer layer from this bamboo stem. I can then eat the softer part inside.

a special, tough lining. This protects it from the splinters in woody bamboo.

I need a lot of energy, so I must eat large amounts of bamboo. I spend about 14 hours a day eating. I sit on my bottom to eat. I hold the bamboo stem in one paw.

I am digging a hole next to a stream to fill it with water. I also get a lot of the water I need from juicy bamboo and even snow.

What Do Pandas Do All Day?

Pandas spend a lot of their day looking for food. They hunt for food in the morning and late afternoon. They must eat regularly, so they spend many hours a day feeding. They even stay up at night to eat!

I sleep on a bed of pine needles to keep warm. I rest my head on my legs or on some tree roots. That helps stop my body from losing heat on the damp ground.

Did You Know?

When bamboo dies, it takes many years to grow back again. That forces me into other forest areas to look for food.

I roll on the ground and rub soil into my belly to keep my fur in good **condition**. The soil soaks up the grease and grime on my fur.

Pandas roll down hills and tumble around. They also roll in the snow, which can help keep their fur in good condition.

When we have plenty to eat, we love to have fun, too.

17

How Do Pandas Talk?

Pandas are very shy and peaceful animals. They prefer to stay away from other pandas and people. Pandas are usually silent, but they do talk to each other by making noises and leaving scent markings.

My scratch and

Did You Know?

Panda cubs cry for attention by making a **high-pitched** sound, just like a human baby.

grunt, grunt

I sniff around to find smelly scent messages from other pandas. That tells me where they live.

Pandas make lots of calls, such as deep roars, barks and low growls. They use these noises to talk to other pandas.

scent marks tell other pandas that this is my territory.

If I stare at you with my head down, I am saying that you are in my territory and I want you to leave.

How Do Pandas Find a Mate?

Female pandas are ready to mate when they are four or five years old. Males are ready to mate when they are six or seven years old. Females have babies only every two or three years. Males will fight noisily over a female they want to mate with.

If I mate

Female pandas attract a male by making deep roars, barks and moans. When a male arrives, the female makes a bleating sound to say she is ready to mate. She sometimes fights males or runs away from them if she is not ready to mate.

We don't really hurt each other when we fight. We just bump and wrestle to find out who is the strongest.

We **breed** in spring. After mating, male pandas leave the females. Females may mate with a few males. They then look for a den in which to have their cubs.

with lots of males, I am more likely to become pregnant.

Did You Know?

Female pandas are pregnant for 97 to 163 days.

How Many Babies Do Pandas Have?

In early autumn, a female panda gives birth to one or two cubs. Just one of the cubs will usually survive. The newborn cubs are so tiny they could fit in the palm of a person's hand. Newborn cubs only weigh as much as a chipmunk. After four weeks the cubs will be 10 times their **birth** weight.

At birth, I was pink, blind and helpless. My black and white fur began to grow after one week.

Did You Know?

Panda mothers are 900 times bigger than their newborn cubs.

I make a den in thick bamboo or in a large, hollow tree. I fill it with leafy branches to make a soft, warm bed for my cubs.

A panda cub is helpless when it is born. Its mother looks after it all the time. She cuddles her cub, even when she sleeps. She licks it clean and feeds it milk every hour.

are newborn, we mew just like a kitten!

SAVE THE PANDA!

It is very difficult to breed pandas in zoos. Why not help a zoo by sponsoring a panda?

How Do Baby Pandas Grow?

When a panda cub is two months old, it opens its eyes for the first time. At three months, the cub's teeth begin to grow through its gums and it begins to crawl. Its mother must still care for it much of the time. By the time the cub is two, it is fully grown.

My mother plays with

Stoats, weasels, golden cats, leopards and wild dogs will attack a panda cub if they find it alone. Mother pandas carry their cubs everywhere in their arms. If they need to move quickly, they carry the cubs in their teeth.

I am four months old.
Look, I can walk now!

me for hours every day.

I ate my first bamboo shoots when I was about six months old. When I am nine months old, I will stop drinking my mother's milk. Then I will feed myself.

Did You Know?

I am ready to leave home when I am about 18 months old.

Can Pandas and People Live Together?

It is illegal to hunt

In 1987, the Chinese government made it **illegal** to hunt pandas. They set up 34 **reserves** in which pandas could live safely. Unfortunately, even pandas living in these areas are still killed by poachers.

Some organizations are trying to help us by building a **corridor** of forest between panda reserves. That will help us travel between reserves to find bamboo and a mate.

me, but many poachers still do.

Every year, more and more people are born in China. They all need somewhere to live. Forests are cut down for wood and to make space for houses. This means that pandas are losing their homes.

SAVE THE PANDA!

We are studied by Chinese scientists. They want to find out how many pandas still live in the wild and what they can do to help us.

Make a donation **to an organization that builds corridors of forest between panda reserves.**

27

What Can You Do to Help Pandas?

There are many organizations trying to help giant pandas to survive in the wild. You can find out more about pandas by looking at the Web sites of organizations that try to help them.

Many people first found out that pandas were in danger in the 1970s, when a type of bamboo started to die out. People all over the world gave money to help pandas. Starving pandas were taken to **refugee camps**, where they were fed and cared for.

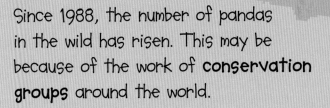

Since 1988, the number of pandas in the wild has risen. This may be because of the work of **conservation groups** around the world.

Why not adopt me?

Find out more about how you can help save pandas and their habitats by visiting this Web site: www.powerkidslinks.com/savethe/panda/

Glossary

bamboo (bam-BOO) A plant with woodlike stems and few leaves.

birth weight (BURTH WAYT) The weight of an animal when first born.

breed (BREED) To make babies.

charity (CHER-uh-tee) A group that gives help to the needy.

condition (kun-DIH-shun) How good or bad something is.

conservation group (kon-sur-VAY-shun GROOP) A group that tries to protect plants or animals.

corridor (KOR-uh-dur) A long, narrow space.

cub (KUB) A baby panda.

donation (doh-NAY-shun) Money given to an organization to help it.

endangered (in-DAYN-jerd) An animal or plant that is in danger of dying out.

habitat (HA-beh-tat) The place where an animal or plant lives.

high-pitched (HY-PICHT) Making a squeaky noise.

illegal (ih-LEE-gul) Against the law.

mate (MAYT) When a male and female animal join to make babies.

organization
(or-guh-nuh-ZAY-shun) A
group of people who work
together.

poacher (POH-cher) Someone
who hunts and kills animals
illegally.

pregnant (PREG-nent) When a
female animal is carrying a
baby inside her.

raccoon (ra-KOON) An animal
with striped markings.

refugee camp (reh-fyoo-JEE
KAMP) A place where
animals or people in trouble
are taken.

reserve (rih-ZURV) An area of
land set aside in which an
animal can live safely.

sea level (SEE LEH-vul) The
level at which the sea meets
the land.

scent (SENT) A smell,
sometimes in liquid form,
made by a plant or animal.

scientist (SY-un-tist) Someone
who uses science to find out
more about the world.

territory (TER-uh-tor-ee) An
area in which an animal lives
and that it protects against
intruders.

waterproof (WAH-ter-proof)
Keeping out water.

Index